D1716143

BE MINDFUL OF MONSTERS

story LAUREN STOCKLY

illustrations ELLEN SURREY

BUMBLE

Ezzy was an adventurous child with an active imagination and emotions so powerful that they seemed like monsters. Ezzy asked certain feelings, like Happiness and Calm, to come and stay as long as they wanted, but told others, like Anger, Worry, Sadness and Fear, to KEEP OUT.

To Ezzy, those uncomfortable feelings were ugly, no-good, stinky, scary monsters. Every time they showed up, Calm was nowhere to be found. When the monsters were lurking nearby, Ezzy's body would begin to tingle. Before long, unpleasant thoughts and memories would start buzzing in Ezzy's mind.

Ezzy was busy getting ready for a big test when Worry crept up from behind. Ezzy tried to hold Worry back, but Worry grew and grew until Ezzy could no longer control it. Ezzy became so distracted that it was impossible to focus on the test.

It used to be easy to fend off Anger. But lately, Anger was around all the time. When Anger stormed in, Ezzy boiled inside and exploded in a rage. With fists clenched, Ezzy yelled and stomped.

Ezzy missed someone special and it hurt too much to think about, so Ezzy put on a fake smile and pretended Sadness was Happiness and everything was fine.

Ezzy tried not to focus on Sadness, but Sadness just wouldn't stop nagging. Soon, Ezzy realized that trying so hard to ignore Sadness made it difficult to notice Happiness. Without either feeling around, the things Ezzy once enjoyed weren't so fun anymore.

When Ezzy's mom went to the store, she assured Ezzy that she would be right back. But as soon as she left, Fear barged in with Worry close behind.

Ezzy thought pretending they weren't there and thinking about all sorts of fun things instead might get them to leave. It helped for a little while, but as soon as the distractions were gone, the monsters reappeared and brought swarms of unpleasant thoughts.

At night, it was hard to fall asleep, and scary dreams left Ezzy with sweaty hands and a pounding heart. Fighting all of the monsters was wearing Ezzy out.

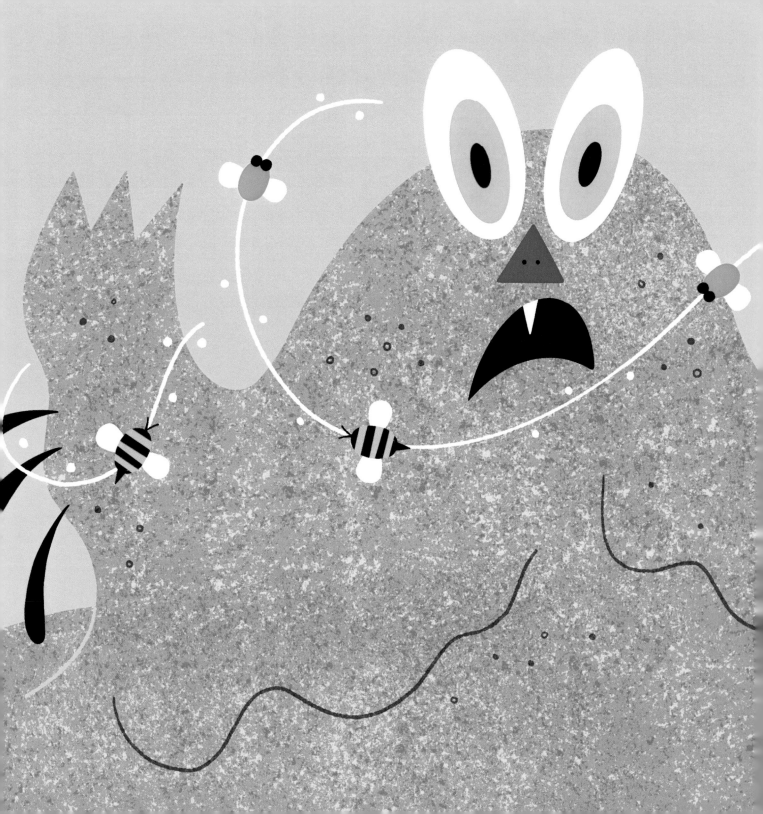

Then one day, all of Ezzy's uncomfortable feelings snuck up at once. Avoiding the feelings had only made them stronger, and now they were all jumbled together, forming the ugliest, stickiest, stinkiest monster Ezzy could imagine.

Ezzy could see parts of Fear, Anger and all of the other monsters in the disgusting ooze. Encountering them all was overwhelming. It felt like sinking in quicksand.

Finally, Ezzy ran to Mom and told her all about the monsters. Mom gave Ezzy a hug and said, "It sounds like those monsters are all of the things you've been holding in lately. They may seem scary, but they're just trying to get help." "You mean they're not dangerous?" asked Ezzy. "They won't harm you," said Mom. "Each one is there for a reason. If you pay close attention and take care of them, they will help you understand what your mind and body need."

Ezzy took another look at the monsters outside, noticing for the first time how lonely and uncomfortable they seemed.

To help take care of the monsters, Mom taught Ezzy about mindfulness, which means paying attention to your thoughts and feelings and accepting them with kindness. Would Ezzy be able to accept such uncomfortable feelings?

Mom shared ways for Ezzy to practice mindfulness, like focusing on each sense and being present in the moment.

Pay close attention to this page and use your senses to name 5 of the tiniest details.

Ezzy also tried taking deep breaths in and out, allowing each thought and feeling to flow. With Calm by Ezzy's side, it was easier to stop fighting the monsters and let them get a little closer.

Ezzy liked to imagine a safe, calm place and do a "butterfly hug." With arms crossed, Ezzy tapped each shoulder one at a time, back and forth in a rhythm.

Ezzy learned that taking care of your body by eating healthy foods, exercising and getting plenty of sleep helps to take care of your feelings too.

Ezzy had never noticed before how emotions make different body parts feel a certain way. But after paying close attention, Ezzy could almost make out some of the messages the monsters were sending.

When the monsters were overwhelming, Ezzy got support from family, friends, other safe adults, and even some imaginary helpers.

Ezzy was finally starting to get better at managing the monsters. But with all of those new skills, could Ezzy get close enough to find out what they really wanted?

Before long, the monsters were lurking again. Ezzy decided to let them get as close as they needed to, remembering that it was okay if they brought up difficult thoughts or memories.

When the monsters arrived, Ezzy welcomed them for a visit. Soon, they started to change. Instead of ugly, menacing beasts, they were little puffy creatures asking for attention. Ezzy was amazed at how terrifying the monsters had seemed before, and how little and harmless they were now.

Ezzy was used to locking away uncomfortable feelings until they would force their way in. But now, Ezzy was beginning to realize that with time and attention, feelings would move along on their own.

Each day, Ezzy made sure to invite feelings in to listen to them and take care of them. Ezzy would play, draw, write, and talk to family and friends. Sometimes the feelings still seemed like monsters and it was hard to accept them, but with practice and patience, Ezzy learned to let them visit a little longer each time.

All along, Ezzy had thought the monsters meant harm, when really they were just trying to help. Anger encouraged Ezzy to speak up and be brave, while Worry reminded Ezzy to be careful.

Fear let Ezzy act fast and stay safe when needed, and Sadness helped Ezzy recognize what was really important. By paying close attention to each feeling, Ezzy began to understand what they were trying to say.

FOR YOURSELF

TAKE A BREAK

ASK FOR SUPPORT

Now when the monsters came, Ezzy would sit with each one, imagining the thoughts and feelings they brought floating gently along, like a wave that would go up and down and then pass right by.

Ezzy was finally mindful of the monsters and ready to accept them, no matter what.

Sad

Disappointed

Lonely

Hurt

Secure

Grateful

Depressed

Numb

Grieving

Silly

Calm

Miserable

How are you feeling?

Loved

Helpless

Confused

Vulnerable

Excited

Happy

Overwhelmed

Proud

Joyful

Hopeful

Peaceful

Relaxed

Safe

Enraged

Frustrated

Disgusted

Insecure

Furious

Jealous

Anxious

Stressed

Anger

Annoyed

Worry

Ashamed

Nervous

Panicked

Shocked

Threatened

Fear

Terrified

LAUREN STOCKLY, LCSW, RPT-S, ECMHS, PPSC is a child and adolescent mental health therapist who specializes in using Play Therapy to treat trauma and support emotional growth for children and families. In addition to her practice, Lauren serves the Play Therapy community as a board member of the California Association for Play Therapy, and shares interventions and resources through her popular blog, CreativePlayTherapist.com. She is also the founder of Bumble BLS, a company dedicated to advancing bilateral stimulation tools for EMDR therapy and emotional regulation in the home.

ELLEN SURREY is an illustrator and designer who's not afraid of using color in her whimsical illustrations. Largely inspired by Mid-Century design and children's books of the 50s and 60s, Ellen enjoys finding beauty in the past and presenting it to a contemporary audience. Her work has appeared in such publications as The New York Times, The New Yorker and The Wall Street Journal. See more of her *work at ellensurrey.com.*

Lauren and Ellen are childhood friends who began writing and illustrating as a team in Kindergarten. They have since refined their talents (and wardrobes), and couldn't be more pleased to share this collaboration rooted in lifelong friendship.

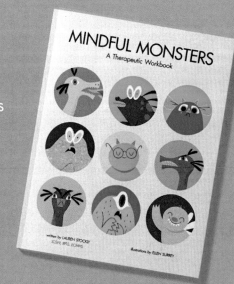

Made in United States
North Haven, CT
21 February 2023

32963846R00024